Conrad Martens, *Sydney Harbour from the residence of Travers*, reproduced with permission of the Dixson Galleries, State Library of New South Wales. Martens looks westward up the Harbour across Milson's Point and Lavender Bay from 'Wotonga', 'Admiralty House'.

We, the People of God at St Mary's (North Sydney, *Cammeray*), St Francis Xavier's (Lavender Bay, *Quiberee*) and Star of the Sea (Kirribilli, *Kiarabilli*) have worshipped on The Other Side for 150 years. We happily acknowledge that our First People, the Cammeragal and their forebears, have sustained their spirits and their bodies in the abundance of this Land, and in their turn have worshipped in these beautiful places for millennia before us.

We hope and pray that we and our First People will be reconciled in the differences that have divided us in the past and that we will share the future with wisdom, grace and justice. Though we live and worship on The Other Side, there is no othersidedness in the Spirit. 'There is neither Jew nor Greek, there is neither slave nor freeman, there is neither male nor female, because you are all one in Christ Jesus' (Galatians 3:28).

We must, by the testimony of our lives, make clear to all the world that it is an integral part of the Christian vocation to bring about a social order 'founded on truth, built on justice and animated by love'.

WITNESSING TO JUSTICE

We feel that we must disagree with those prophets of gloom, who are always forecasting disaster, as though the end of the world was at hand. In the present order of things, Divine Providence is leading us to a new order of human relations which, by humanity's own efforts and even beyond those very expectations, are directed toward the fulfilment of God's superior and inscrutable designs. And everything, even human differences, leads to the greater good of the Church.

OPENING ADDRESS OF POPE JOHN XXIII TO VATICAN COUNCIL II, 11 OCTOBER 1962

Since once again, Lord, I have neither bread nor wine, nor altar, I will raise myself beyond these symbols, up to the pure majesty of the real itself; I, your priest, will make the whole earth my altar and on it will offer you all the labours and sufferings of the world.

HYMN OF THE UNIVERSE

Pedro Arrupe SJ, 28th General of the Society of Jesus 1965–1983 challenged his Jesuits to reform themselves according to the radical message of Christ in the modern world.

Blessed John XXIII (1881–1963) gave the Church the freedom to be its modern self with his hopefulness infused with faith.

Teilhard de Chardin SJ (1881–1955) visionary Jesuit palaeontologist whose spiritual writings were banned by the Church and the Jesuits in his lifetime but whose sense of the Divine infusing the universe from the beginning of evolutionary time inspired many in Vatican Council II and would be often quoted by Pope John Paul II.

PARISH PRIESTS—ST MARY'S

Dr Peter Powell	1856–1867
Dean John Kenny	1867–1878
Joseph Dalton SJ	1878–1879
James Kennedy SJ	1880–1882
Michael Kelly SJ	1883–1889
Oliver Daly SJ	1890–1892
Joseph Brennan SJ	1893–1901
George Kelly SJ	1902–1909
James Colgan SJ	1910–1912
Edward Corish SJ	1913–1917
Joseph Hearne SJ	1918–1921
Dominic Connell SJ	1922–1928
Richard O'Mara SJ	1929–1947
Arthur Stone SJ	1948–1953
Henry Johnston SJ	1954–1956
George Collopy SJ	1957–1961
Thomas Costelloe SJ	1962–1970
James Dynon SJ	1971–1974
Paul Coleman SJ	1975–1985
George Belfrage SJ	1986–1987
Joseph Sobb SJ	1988–1992
Peter Quin SJ	1993–2004
Anthony Smith SJ	2004–

ST FRANCIS XAVIER'S, STAR OF THE SEA

Parish Priests	1922–1990
Richard Murphy SJ	1922–1925
James Magan SJ	1926–1931
Patrick McGrath SJ	1932–1943
Arthur Stone SJ	1944–1948
Richard O'Mara SJ	1949
John O'Shaughnessy SJ	1950–1953
Arthur Stone SJ	1954–1959
Thomas Costelloe SJ	1960–1961
Kevin Staunton SJ	1962–1970
Denis Sheridan SJ	1971–1973
Robert Walsh SJ	1973–1983
Peter Quin SJ	1983–1988
Celso Romanin SJ	1989–1990

ST MARY'S SCHOOL, NORTH SYDNEY

School Principals

MARIST BROTHERS

Brother Walter Moore	1888–1890
Brother Francis Mullins	1891–1895
Brother Clement Murray	1895–1897
Brother Osmund Rice	1897–1899
Brother Philip Jeffreys	1899–1900
Brother Thomas Ludeke	1901–1906
Brother Gilbert O'Donoghue	1907–1912
Brother Casmir O'Shaughnesssy	1913–1915

SISTERS OF ST JOSEPH

Sister Donatus Egan	1916–1925
Sister Benizi Casey	1926–1929
Sister Placida Kiss	1930–1935
Sister Cordula McManus	1936–1946
Sister Miriam Gittens	1947–1954

SISTERS OF MERCY

Sister M Pauline Devine	1955–1961
Sister M. John Conant	1962
Sister M Adrian	1963–1965
Sister M. John Conant	1966–1968
Sister Francis M. Whelan	1969–1975
Sister M Nicholas Gillies	1976–1977
Sister M. Peter Chanel McMillan	1978–1980
Sister Ellen Cahill	1981–1988

LAY PRINCIPALS

Mrs Susan Clifton	1989–1994
Mrs Frances Garrett	1995–2002
Mrs Rosemary DeBono	2003–

There is an arithmetic of salvation. Churches are great counters—of the baptised, the married, the dead, of communions given, confessions heard, sick visited, of members of pious societies and sodalities, of Easter dues paid. The annual bishop's visitations of all the churches in the world will keep recording angels on the Last Day hard at work for a considerable part of eternity.

So a 150 years' story of the parishes on The Other Side will always begin with a register. Mostly 40 cm long, 31 cm wide and 6 cm deep, 82 volumes in number, registers line the shelves of St Mary's archives. They are precious and are carefully looked after by the parish archivist, Barney Mungoven. There will be thousands of requests to check a detail that will be important in someone's life.

Let's begin with the first register, the Marriage Register for 1856–1868.

17 April 1856. Bernard Daly, a 39 year-old, Irish-born widower with no children, innkeeper by trade, marries Catherine Collins, 26-year-old spinster, also Irish-born. Residences, North Shore and Pittwater. John Collins and Ellen Head are their witnesses. The registers will give their fathers' occupations and their mothers' maiden names, Bridget Geogheghan his, Catherine Roche, hers. All can sign their names. It will be a rare marriage in these early years that doesn't have someone simply give his or her mark (X).

Diligent and generous friends, who would be embarrassed to have their names known, have counted 183 170 items in these registers. They tell us that there will be 14 600 marriages through the 150 years of the three churches of this first North Shore parish. So we have the names, birthplace (mostly Ireland in these early days), age (mostly in the mid- and late 20s), occupation (builder, stonemason, servant, cook, rope maker, sailor, housekeeper, seamstress…) of 29 200 men and women. Almost the same information for a further 29 200 witnesses and the same again for 58 400 parents. 116 800 in total. That is enough—but not here—for a social and cultural portrait of the parish.

Our friends counted 21 107 infant and 1556 adult baptisms as well. More than 100 000 men, women and children would have called themselves parishioners through these years. And 133 priests served their sacramental and spiritual needs. Sisters of Mercy, of St Joseph, of Loreto, Marist Brothers and The Grail served their educational and social needs. The parishioners, in their turn, helped them build their schools, hospitals, orphanages and refuges, as well as eight versions of their own churches with unending generosity.

These parishioners and their parish servants have lived their faith and worshipped through two world wars, several depressions, federation, national and international turmoil. The Bridge transformed their North Shore and the Warringah Expressway divided their parish. A high rise Central Business District took the heart out of their living space. Their priests at one time knew all their names and visited them in their homes. Now, as they move into their sesquicentenary, the parish is a parish without boundaries. Faithful from 75 postcodes come to their Sunday Masses.

POPES	
Pius IX	1846–1878
Leo XIII	1878–1903
Pius X	1903–1914
Benedict XV	1914–1922
Pius XI	1922–1939
Pius XII	1939–1958
John XXIII	1958–1963
Paul VI	1963–1978
John Paul	1978
John Paul II	1978–2005
Benedict XVI	2005–

JESUIT GENERALS	
John Roothaan SJ	1829–1853
Peter Beckx SJ	1853–1887
Anton Maria Anderley SJ	1887–1892
Louis Martin SJ	1892–1906
Frances Xavier Wernz SJ	1906–1915
Wlodimir Ledochowski SJ	1915–1946
John Baptist Janssens SJ	1946–1965
Pedro Arrupe SJ	1965–1983
Peter-Hans Kolvenbach SJ	1983–

SYDNEY ARCHBISHOPS	
John Bede Polding OSB	1842–1877
Roger Bede Vaughan OSB	1877–1883
Patrick Francis Cardinal Moran	1884–1911
Michael Kelly	1911–1940
Norman Thomas Cardinal Gilroy	1940–1971
James Darcy Cardinal Freeman	1971–1983
Edward Bede Cardinal Clancy	1983–2001
George Cardinal Pell	2001–

THE BRIDGE

Frank Cash, the pastor of Christ Church, Lavender Bay, had a spiritual engagement with the Bridge. He photographed every day in its building and nearly every bolt and girder in its structure. In *Parables of the Sydney Harbour Bridge* (1930) he sees the Bridge through a myriad of scriptural texts and calls the Bridge a 'sacramental sign — an 'outward expression of an inward facility' of humanity to originate a design and materialise it. Father Patrick McGrath SJ, parish priest of St Francis Xavier's, officially blessed the Bridge in the days before its dramatic opening. The Bridge would change The Other Side forever. Father McGrath prayed it would be for the good.

^ Grace Cossington Smith, Australia 1892–1984. *The bridge in-curve* (1930) tempera on cardboard, 83.6 x 111.8 cm. Presented by the National Gallery Society of Victoria, 1967, National Gallery of Victoria, Melbourne.

< Construction of the Warringah Expressway. By permission of the Stanton Library. Photo John Early Pty. Ltd.

⌄ Sydney Harbour Bridge. Children's Day, 16 March 1932. Photo *Sydney Mail*.

Warringah Expressway cut a swathe through the parish. Well over a thousand residents lost their place of abode. Some attempt was made to offset the skewed nature of the now divided parish by having the Jesuits accept responsibility for St Joseph's, Neutral Bay. From 1991–2000, Celso Romanin SJ, Andrew Zerafa SJ, Donal Taylor SJ, Patrick Bishop SJ and Robert Walsh SJ served the combined parishes of Star of the Sea, Kirribilli, and St Joseph's, Neutral Bay.

The Children's March on 16 March 1932, three days before the opening of the Bridge, saw 50 000 school children march across the Bridge. The girls and boys of St Francis Xavier's School were reputed to have led the march.

^ Francis Xavier in his niche.
Photo Robyn Treseder.
> Our Lady of the Way, Lavender Bay.
Photo Robyn Treseder.
ᵛ Mary in Australian landscape. Courtesy
Peter Norden SJ, Jesuit Social Services.

ST MARY'S We reverence the Mother of God in the ancient title of St Mary's as one of us, as one of the communion of saints. As St Mary, she is Miriam of Nazareth, the young Jewish girl who said to God 'Thy will be done', the 50-year-old woman who bore the pain of her son's terrible death. In a year in which the Anglican and Roman communions seek to discover what unites them and what divides them in their devotion to Mary, St Mary's is also a very ecumenical title.

STAR OF THE SEA We do not know why Star of the Sea was added to St Mary's on the foundation stone of the first church. Pius IX proclaimed the doctrine of the Immaculate Conception in 1854, just two years before the foundation stone was laid, and official documents tell us that the Feast of the Immaculate Conception (8 December) is the patronal day of St Mary's in North Sydney. We suspect that Dr Powell as he erected his tent high on a hill and along a street that would be called Ridge could see the harbour if he looked south and the Heads if he looked east. Star of the Sea would be a welcoming shrine in this land of travellers, migrants and mariners.

The name Star of the Sea became more immediately pertinent when the Jesuits acquired the Congregational church on the edge of the Harbour at Milson's Point in 1880. They erected a statue of Our Lady, Star of the Sea, and put it in front of the church looking out on what we now call Circular Quay. We have that statue still, in the quadrangle of St Aloysius College.

OUR LADY OF THE WAY The Jesuits have had a devotion to *Our Lady of the Way* ever since they were given, in 1540 at the time of their foundation, the small wayside chapel, Santa Maria della Strada, that housed this painting. That chapel is now the great Baroque Church of the Gesu in Rome. Some form of the image of Our Lady of the Way is to be found in all our churches in the parish. The Way, the Jesuits will tell you, is their Jesuit way of Ignatian Spirituality, but they also like the notion that life is a pilgrimage that needs shrines of some sort.

ST FRANCIS XAVIER'S Xavier is the personification of a Jesuit passion for translation and entry into others' lives through their own cultural metaphors, whether they are Indian, Indonesian, Japanese or Moluccan. Xavier entered all those cultures in the last ten extraordinary years of his life. He also saw the world through the eyes of the poor. The name St Francis Xavier's is an icon of mission and compassion.

^ In this 1878 Bernard Holtermann photograph, the vacant two acres the Jesuits bought for St Francis Xavier's can be seen beyond St Peter's Presbyterian Church. Courtesy Mitchell Library, State Library of NSW.

> St Mary's Old Stone Church. Sanctuary on east end of church on Miller Street. Note the tramlines. St Mary's Archives.

˅ Looking north over Bennelong Point to 'Kirribilli Point'. The then Congregational Church (1870) can be seen centre left. Courtesy Mitchell Library, State Library of NSW.

> Dr Peter Powell, first parish priest, 1856–1867.

^ A map of the early parish drawn by Mr E. Roy for Henry Johnston SJ's centenary history, *A Seed that Grew.*

> This bell, the gift of the retired Auditor-General William Lithgow, has rung the *angelus* at St Mary's every day since 1862.

ᵛ Archpriest John Therry said the first home Masses in the parish in Berry Street on this chest of drawers and before this crucifix. The Mass chest is presently in the sanctuary at St Mary's.

The Reverend Dr Peter Powell is a good horseman. He will need to be. The North Shore parish he will pioneer reaches north to the Pitt Water, east to the coast from Palm Beach to Manly, west to what we now call Lane Cove. His six feet make a fine figure in the saddle. He is a charismatic preacher with a racy Irish humour. In a time of much church and school building and furnishing, this was prized and bishops would use his charisma wherever he went to raise funds. The Reverend Doctor played a mean fiddle, too, had a fine voice and was handsome. That helped.

Dr Powell came to Sydney in 1855. He had lived ten years in the colonies before then. During that time he pioneered parishes in Guildford WA, Penola and Mt Gambier in SA, Heidelberg, Geelong and Keilor in Victoria. He had been president of a seminary, inspector of schools, and founder and prior to a monastery with the unlikely name of 'Hippo' in Campbellfield, Victoria. The first eleven years of the parish of North Sydney will mark his longest posting.

A group of Catholic laity, led by Nicholas and Mary (Larkin) Pyne, had been conniving with the help of Archpriest John Joseph Therry, a perpetual pest of bishops and apostle for religious and political liberty, to establish a parish on the North Shore.

A Mr Daly of the Union Inn had been eyeing the vacant two acres of Lots 7, 8, 9 and 10 of Section 16. They were cleared land on top of the highest hill nearest the harbour. A government grant of the land would do them fine.

Powell is a fast worker. First he has a tent set up for Mass and has the land planted with maize for his horse. Then he builds the first wooden church of St Mary's Star of the Sea. Archbishop John Bede Polding OSB blesses it on 13 March 1856.

St Mary's Star of the Sea is 10 metres by 20 metres. The walls are 3 metres high and tree-trunk pillars support the shingle roof. Wallpaper covers the roughness of it all. The floor is earthen, covered by rushes and bracken. There are three rows of pew—still to be found at the rear of the present St Mary's—but no kneelers. It is prickly kneeling, and in those days there is plenty of kneeling. The roof does not do much of a job in a Sydney rainstorm. Then the floor is an estuary of muddy streams. The altar, against centuries of tradition in the Church, is at the western end. The entrance is at the eastern end, off Miller Street.

Dr Powell leaves St Mary's somewhat hurt and discouraged and in a hurry in 1867. His parishioners do not appreciate his spending their money on yet another tent from which the overflow of Sunday Masses could see proceedings through the side windows of the wooden church.

^ > Dean John Kenny, parish priest 1867–1878, and the first stone church, which Dean Kenny planned.

^ Alma Cottage, much renovated. Dean Kenny gave the cottage to the Sisters of St Joseph to establish themselves on the North Shore.

ⱽ Dean Kenny's terrace houses on Mount Street around which a convent, a chapel and then a museum and shrine of Blessed Mary MacKillop grew.

Dean John Kenny is Dr Powell's successor. Dean Kenny is a Scotsman, possessed of gentle piety, a generous heart and something of the intellectual passion of the Scottish Enlightenment. He was to write *A History of the Commencement and Progress of Catholicity in Australia up to the year 1840* (Sydney, 1886). It is notable for a sympathetic and scholarly appendix on the Aborigines.

Dean Kenny changes the altar of the wooden church to the eastern end and plans a new stone church.

He would make a large impact on the North Shore. When he makes way for the Jesuits in 1878, he retires to his 'Alma Cottage', high on the hill above Blue's Point, as the point was called then, 'Wallumetta' now. There he would give great comfort to Mother Mary MacKillop and her Josephites, making it possible for them to establish their novitiate there. He leaves them, in his will, the terrace houses he owned on Mount Street. These houses are transformed and enlarged through the decades into a convent, a chapel, a museum and the final resting place of the Blessed Mary.

The global Church was attracting the attention in these years of the NSW population, Catholic or not. Pius IX publishes the *Syllabus of Errors* in 1864 and calls Vatican Council I in 1869. A future Cardinal of Sydney, Patrick Francis Moran, writes the definition of papal infallibility. Garibaldi begins his marches. The pope is 'prisoner of the Vatican'. The whole Catholic world confuses Pius IX's political diplomacy with the Faith and comes to his rescue. In 1858, a young 14-year-old girl, Bernadette Soubiroux, has the first of 18 mysterious visions.

In Australia, 1862 saw the advent of the 'Irish bishops'. They had little respect for the English Benedictine Archbishop of Sydney, Roger Vaughan OSB, and he next to none for them. The Irish bishops come, via Rome, from an Irish church that was about to be 'Romanised' by Bishop (later Cardinal) Paul Cullen of Dublin. He would build a thousand chapels and then flood the traditional practices with an imported piety of novenas, sodalities, benedictions, processions, and missions. And religious things: beads, scapulars, medals, holy pictures.

The Irish bishops and the priests that came with them and after them spend £1 million on churches and schools in NSW between 1866 and 1879. Let's say $115 million in current funds. Meanwhile Vaughan doubles the number of churches and chapels in his archdiocese in ten years.

There is a passion in the faithful that the priests and bishops are tapping. The generosity of these mostly poorer people is extraordinary. Because they feel beleaguered in the colony they build generously and endlessly. *Their* churches, *their* schools, *their* presbyteries and halls are sacramentals of their Catholic identity.

The Jesuits come to Sydney with drive. Father Therry makes it happen. Posthumously. He leaves them £14 000, about $2 million in current terms. Not any sort of Jesuits. Austrian Jesuits have been in South Australia since 1848. Irish Jesuits. Therry wants Irish Jesuits. The Irish Jesuits do him proud. They send out a talented 49-year-old man of vision and energy, Joseph Dalton SJ (1817–1905) to lead, them.

What Dalton does with that £14 000 is little short of amazing. It gives him credit with banks to restore St Patrick's College, East Melbourne; to buy 70 acres for Xavier College and begin its building; establish parishes in Richmond and Hawthorn.

He comes to Sydney in 1878, and immediately acquires 118 acres for Riverview College in Lane Cove, St Kilda House in Woolloomooloo for the first St Aloysius College. He buys two acres of empty land at Lavender Bay and a small, empty Independent Church at Milson's Point. He builds a church–school, which we know as St Francis Xavier's.

Jesuits are viewed suspiciously by seculars and Protestants in these years and are expelled from a dozen countries. But they come to Sydney in triumph as the Catholic Church's greatest educators and apologists. That is what Archbishop Vaughan wants. Educators whose standards cannot be questioned. He wants apologists and debaters too, to fill the halls and argue against Protestants. The times are here, he knows, when the faithful are in need of more spiritual sustenance than the mere religious basics. They need missions, retreats, devotions. The many congregations of religious women in the archdiocese need spiritual counselling. He needs canon lawyers, theologians and spiritual directors, and gets them.

Dalton brings James Kennedy SJ with him to Sydney and sets him up as St Mary's parish priest. He and Dalton establish a 'presbytery' on West Street, a shack half made of flattened kerosene tins. Dalton and Kennedy begin pastoral life enthusiastically. Dalton says the 8 a.m. and 11 a.m. Mass at St Mary's on their first Sunday. Kennedy says the 9 a.m. Mass at the church–school they inherit at Pymble 19 kilometres away. There are devotions to Mary and benediction in the evening. They begin their work at St Mary's with a fortnight retreat: first week for the children and adolescents, second week for adults. Mass and sermon in the morning. Rosary and meditation in the evening.

Almost immediately the North Shore knows that in the Jesuits they are in touch with the worldwide church. Brilliant orators from the USA visit them. They come in strength—to Riverview and St Aloysius as well as to the North Shore.

∧ The altar of the old stone church of St Mary's with the 1880 paintings of the Misses Zahel on each side. Joseph Brennan SJ, parish priest 1893–1901, added the transepts to the then eastward — and Miller Street — oriented church, 1896, just before the second — and westward directed — stone church replaced it, 1898–1938.

< Joseph Dalton SJ, parish priest 1878–1879.

∨ The Jesuits built this Shrine to Our Lady of the Way in the first stone church in the 1880s.

^ In the top left-hand corner of the photograph Monte Sant' Angelo can be seen. In 1879 the Sisters of Mercy had bought Mr Francis Lord's property that stretched from Miller Street to Lane Cove Road (now the Pacific Highway).

500m out of sight on the top of the photograph is St Joseph's Convent and Blessed Mary MacKillop's Shrine. Further along on the top edge can be seen 'Avila', the headquarters of the Grail on McHattan Street.

Move to the top right edge of the photo. Mater Misericordiae Private Hospital is to be found 500m off the photo. From 1906 when the Sisters of Mercy established a cottage hospital until 1982 when it ceased as a public hospital, and now as a Private Hospital, the Mater, with its sisters, doctors and nurses, has been a focus of Catholic compassion both to the parish and from the parish.

Down the right side of the photograph and again 200m off on the corner of West and Hayberry Streets was in 1856, the farm of Mr Lithgow who left his bell to St Mary's.

It is difficult to keep memory alive in old buildings and in landscapes. Plaques and memorials help. Story does, too. But they all need the theatre or ritual to breath life into them.

^ St Mary's sanctuary before the changes of the 1970s following Vatican II. Photo St Mary's Archives.

> A.M.D.G., *Ad Maiorem Dei Gloriam*, 'To the Greater Glory of God', the Jesuit signature on sacred spaces and life, and no doubt heading millions on millions of pages in school exercise books in times past. Photo Robyn Treseder.

v St Mary's. Photo Robyn Treseder.

Let's pretend we have X-ray vision as we try to see the past in the 1989 aerial photo opposite, presented by the Marist Brothers to the Jesuit Fathers as the Marists celebrated their centenary in the parish.

The perspective of the photograph is from the north. It shows the block on which St Mary's has stood for 150 years. Miller Street is along the left side to the east, Carlow Street along the bottom, West Street on the right and Ridge Street along the top of the block.

Go to the left edge of the photo. The North Sydney oval is peeking out of what since 1879 we know as St Leonard's Park. The foresighted first Mayor of St Leonard's (North Sydney), Alderman William Tunks, planned its 16.2 hectares and paced out all its paths. Indeed he tragically died there, falling into a well under construction. In 1856 the bushland stretched for kilometres. The bird life was prolific until hunters shot it out of the sky. Priests from the parish were known to get lost in the bush.

Peer through the bitumen of Miller Street. You will see tramlines. A cable tram ran from Milson's Point to its terminus on the corner of Miller and Ridge Streets from 1886 to 1900, when it was electrified. The lines were pulled out in 1958. The schedule of trams that eventually ran from the Spit Junction along Military Road, up Miller Street and down to Milson's Point affected Mass times—Mass began 10 minutes after the hour. The obligation of Sunday Mass attendance was measured precisely in those days—from the Offertory to Communion. Older parishioners might remember that the back of the church began to get crowded as the sermon ended!

The present St Mary's (1938–) on the corner of Miller and Ridge is a compound of all the churches on the site: the wooden church (1856–1868, also a church-school 1856–1860); the first stone church (1868–1898, enlarged in 1896); and the second stone church (1898–1938). The outer stone wall of the present St Mary's is the stone from the second stone church, as are some of the stained-glass windows and the sanctuary marble in the Shrine of Our Lady of the Way. Paintings by the pioneer parishioners, the Misses Zahel, are to be seen in the church.

The church–school for boys and girls moved in 1860 to the Pyne's house on Miller Street (top left in photo). The great schoolteacher of the parish, Jeremiah Crowley, ran it. It moved again off the photo to the corner of William and Mount Streets (1862–1882), then it came back to Ridge Street (behind St Mary's in the photo), where for 142 years it has had changing educational modes.

The Marist Brothers School began in 1888 for the rapidly developing working-class area of North Sydney. In 1913, with 300 students, the school was moved to Mark Foy's Repository on Carlow Street which Father Edward Corish SJ had converted into classrooms and a hall, named Manresa. Manresa was a small town near Barcelona where Ignatius Loyola composed his *Spiritual Exercises*. The Sisters of St Joseph then took over the Ridge Street building as a girls and infants school and set up their convent in the residence beside it. In 1962, the Wyndham Scheme was introduced into NSW education and the Brother's School needed refurbishment. Father Tom Costelloe SJ saw to the building of a new school and library at the cost of £90 000. He thus began 20 years of development on the site north of the presbytery. In 1981 with a Commonwealth Schools Commission Grant of $125 000 and $35 000 from the parish, land was bought and a new building erected. Father Paul Coleman SJ acquired more land for a playground and extension of the south building of the school. Loans and contributions from the parish and parents raised the $672 349 necessary. Manresa Hall

had been condemned as a school building by the Education Department and was demolished. The amphitheatre, built of bricks from the demolition can be seen on what is known as 'The O'Mara Green', in honour of Richard O'Mara SJ, parish priest from 1928 to 1947 and builder of the present St Mary's. The parish built a 'monastery' that the brothers occupied in 1916.

Dr Powell had owned one of the terrace houses north of the school on Miller Street. He sold it to a pioneer family of the parish: the Zahels.

The Sisters of Mercy come to the parish in 1873 and opened up a day and boarding school just visible in the aerial photograph on the northern corner of Carlow and West Streets.

That vacant spot on Carlow Street with the basketball court markings will certainly have phantoms. Maybe not of the opera, but certainly of boxing and housie, of an occasional musical like *Song of Bernadette*, and lots of amateur productions and school concerts. It is where Manresa Hall stood from 1913 to 1982. The thespian spirit of the parish lived there for 69 years.

West Street was the site of the Jesuits' first kerosene-tin presbytery. Dr Powell had lived there, too, in 'Palmyra' and 'Mellifont'. Since 1967 the Jesuit Mission Centre has occupied a cottage at no. 31. It came from 34 Ridge Street, where since 1956 Eileen Madden and her workers had run an opportunity shop.

< Richard O'Mara SJ, parish priest 1929–1947.

^ Brothers Walter, Michael and Wilfred with the first pupils of the Marist Brothers School 1888.

< Edward Corish SJ (right), parish priest 1913–1917, and Edward Sydes SJ, St Mary's 1910–1916.

ˇ Manresa Hall up ...

< Grace Cossington Smith, *The curve of the Bridge*, 1928–29, oil on cardboard, 110.5 x 82.5 cm. Purchased with funds provided by the Art Gallery Society of New South Wales and James Fairfax 1991. Collection: Art Gallery of New South Wales. © estate of Grace Cossington Smith. Photography: Jenni Carter for AGNSW.

∧ Star of the Sea, Milson's Point. Courtesy St Aloysius Archives.

∨ Manresa Hall coming down.

^ This photograph of the altar and its statues, its rails and cloth, and with the tabernacle giving a focus to anyone entering the church, gives us an image of the Catholic imagination pre-Vatican Council II.

> This strong image of the Virgin as Star of the Sea stood overlooking the harbour for many years. Lit up at night, it was a welcoming beacon to ferry-riders landing at Milson's Point.

∨ St Aloysius College came to Milson's Point in 1903. Star of the Sea was still facing the Harbour at that time. In 1940 Miss Angela Hepburn generously supported internal and external renovations. The entrance from then on was off Pitt Street.

George Alfred Lloyd of 'Wotonga' (now Admiralty House) donates a piece of land on Clapham Rise, as Pitt Street was known then, for the erection of a Congregational Church. On 20 April 1863, as we know from a copy of the *Sydney Morning Herald* preserved in a jar in the foundations, his daughter 'with a chastely wrought silver trowel gracefully performed the ceremony of laying the stone'.

The first pastor did not work out, and the congregation moved en masse to St Thomas, North Sydney. To the chagrin of many who thought it 'traitorous to our denomination', the Jesuits were happy to buy the empty church in 1880 for £1650.

A great crowd is present to see the blessing and opening of Star of the Sea. They interrupt the speeches of William Kelly SJ and Archbishop Vaughan with much applause. Education is on the Archbishop's mind.

The newspapers refer sardonically to the 'fashionable' and 'aristocratic' character of the church's environment. But the parishioners are mostly Irish working-class and their houses small. They would suffer most when the building of the bridge destroyed 438 of their homes, and the Warringah Expressway 450.

The Jesuits bring St Aloysius from the South Shore to the North Shore in 1903 and Star of the Sea becomes virtually a school chapel.

Through the 1950s Cardinal Gilroy was urging the Jesuits to take more interest in Kirribilli. Many parishioners were dismayed when a church so special to them was demolished in 1978 with the expansion of St Aloysius College.

We have a church, St Francis Xavier's, born of a remarkable man's vision. William Wilkinson Wardell (1823–1899) designed St Patrick's Cathedral in Melbourne and in Hobart, St Mary's Cathedral in Sydney, St John's College at the University of Sydney, St Ignatius in Richmond, Government House in Melbourne and many other buildings, as well as St Francis Xavier's. As a young man in England he was tutored in architecture by Augustus Pugin and inspired by John Henry Newman. He followed Newman into the Church. Poor health brought him to the colonies in 1858. 'Black Wednesday', the sacking of all Victorian public servants, brought him to Sydney at the same time as the Jesuits in 1878. It was natural that Joseph Dalton SJ, having benefited from Wardell's brilliance at St Ignatius, Richmond, would ask him to design the Jesuits first church on the North Shore.

Wardell would be comfortable, we have to think, in a Vatican Council II Church, as Newman inspired many of Vatican Council II's themes. One was the spiritual union of the Church across all its expressions. Another was the continuity of the Church from its earliest times to the present, woven in its tradition. New Gothic, Wardell's style of architecture, was not just that, a style. It was a revival movement. St Francis Xavier's, in Wardell's hope for it, would have been a repository in its spaces of the Church's millennial truths and of the Church's eternal call to goodness.

∧ The high-rises begin to crowd in.
Photo Robyn Treseder.

∨ St Francis Xavier's brand-new in 1881.
Its gleaming stone was quarried locally.
Photo B. Holtermann. Courtesy of the Mitchell
Library, State Library of NSW.

^ William Wilkinson Wardell's beautiful church.

^ Sydney Harbour being a dangerous place in the Second World War, the parishioners built air-raid shelters for the children at St Francis Xavier's School.

ᵛ Richard Murphy SJ's tennis courts.

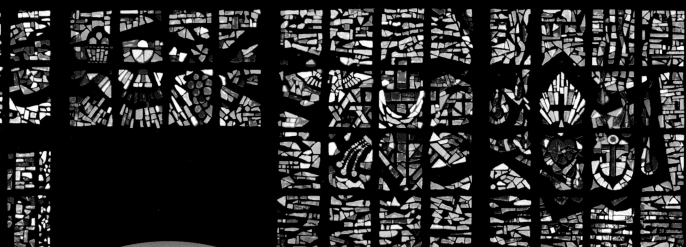

^ 35-metre Loire glass wall at St Francis Xavier's designed by Stephen Moor. Photo Peter Melocco.

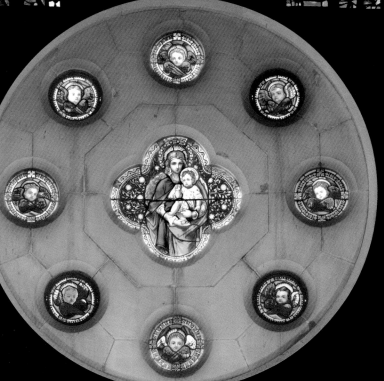

^ Rose, western wall, St Francis Xavier's. Photo Peter Melocco.

<^ Concelebrated Mass for the centenary of the coming of the Jesuits to the parish, 1981.

Colonial realities were harsh on inspirational architecture. For 20 years these sacred spaces were also classrooms — the best in Sydney, Jeremiah Crowley, the school's principal, thought. They were even a small museum! This was a Jesuit building. In 1901, the school moved out of the church to what is now — through many changes in the 1930s and '40s — the Leo XIII building.

< Kevin Staunton SJ, parish priest Lavender Bay, 1962–1970. Father Staunton, here wearing his RSL badge, was a commando in the Second World War and was wounded by a grenade in Crete. He had the changes he made in the church listed as a war memorial.

Parish priests and progress tend not to have much time for architects' dreams. Progress in the form of a railway tunnel and station destroyed the comfortable double entry to the church and school property off Blue Street. Richard Murphy SJ, the first parish priest of an independent St Francis Xavier's was an A-Grade tennis player. He thought the land in front of the church, nicely landscaped with pepper trees, would be better used as tennis courts. James Magan SJ, who had been a chaplain in Flanders Fields and gave the Parish Bulletin one of its more creative titles, *Priceless*, had little time for Wardell's Gothic simplicity inside the church. He favoured a more colourful Irish devotionalism. He painted a mural of the Canadian Martyrs on the wall behind the altar, coloured in the truly priceless stations, and joined them with a painted frieze of waratahs, daisies and thorns. Tom Costelloe SJ thought he might be exiled when he painted over the frieze.

^ James Magan SJ, also returned from service in the First World War as a chaplain. Here are his decorations to the altar.

ᵛ And here is how Father Staunton cleaned Father Magan's decorations up.

From 1922 to 1962, a period of growing family population in the parish, there was talk of enlarging St Francis Xavier's or of building a second church on the property alongside Miller Street which the Jesuits had bought and sold and bought back again at different times. It was Kevin Staunton SJ, a parish priest always hard-pressed between the pressures of Cardinal Gilroy to expand the parish and the reluctance of the Jesuit provincial to have the Society laboured with its debts, who enlarged the church neither forward or backward, nor up nor down, but sideways. William Wardell no doubt wept a little in his grave at what this did to his church, and every parish priest that has followed has had a problem with the skewed spaces inside that resulted, but Father Staunton thought he could silence criticism with something spectacular, a 35-metre Loire glass wall, the longest in the world at the time. Stephen Moor designed it. At the same time the exquisite 1860s artistry of the master-carver, Josef Dettlinger of Freiburg-on-Breslau was rediscovered by stripping the Stations of Father Magan's gaudy paint. Sid Acret, a parishioner, had the arduous and delicate task of stripping the carvings.

'Wangan' on MacKenzie Street, the property and mansion home of the MacKenzie family since 1874, was bought by the Jesuits in 1913 as a presbytery, now a Parish Centre. They enlarged it, inevitably more usefully than gracefully.

^'Wangan' and additions.

^Star of the Sea, Kirribilli.
Photo Peter Melocco.

^ Loire glass wall, tabernacle and baptistery.
(above) and altar and sanctuary (below).
Photos Peter Melocco.

Sailing ships used to be careened in 'Careening Bay'. A Star of the Sea Church would not be inappropriate there. Kirribilli—*Kiarabilli,* 'Good Fishing Spot'—sounds like the advice the Lord gave to his apostles on Lake Galilee (Luke 5:4–7). Star of the Sea, Kirribilli, will do.

The parish came to this quiet spot thinking to break the psychological and physical isolation, indeed the depression, following the demolition of the Milson's Point site. The Spirit seemed to be at work in a referendum in the local community that went against the building of an RSL club on already cleared land. The parish sold the built-on blocks it owned on the south side of Willoughby Street, and bought the present site.

Star of the Sea would be architecturally a post-Vatican II church. So the altar is turned around and is a simple communion table. The baptismal font is in the front of the church so that the whole community can participate in baptisms of a Sunday. The tabernacle is no longer the focal point, but belongs to a small side Blessed Sacrament chapel. Its Loire glass wall is Father Staunton's signature on the church.

Cardinal Gilroy blessed and opened the Star of the Sea on 25 June 1970. He moved between Cana and the barque of St Peter on stormy waters in his homily. He said the Votive Mass of Our Lady, Star of the Sea and the congregation sang an old, nostalgic hymn 'Ave Maris Stella' (Hail Queen of Heaven, Ocean Star) with fervour. In an effort to calm somewhat the stormy waters of a post-Vatican II Church and to offset the strangeness of this new sacred space, an altar without altar rails, the people were told that they were free to receive communion standing or kneeling.

^ Kevin Staunton SJ offering Mass for the intentions of the donors to St Francis Xavier's renovations, 1964.

> Catholic Truth Society pamphlets. The *Penny Catechism*, *Madonna* and the *Messenger of the Sacred Heart* were only some of the supports for the faith in the pre-Vatican II Church.

˅ Des Dwyer SJ, John Raper, Pastoral Assistant, and children. Photo Robyn Treseder.

It is 1956, the parish's centennial year. Parish priest, Henry Johnston SJ publishes his history of the first 100 years, *The Seed that Grew*. Twenty-four parishes, that had evolved out of the one North Shore parish that Dr Powell had established, lead a procession around St Leonard's Park. St Mary's gets a new white stone pulpit with Dr Powell's and Dean Kenny's names inscribed on it. Cardinal Gilroy celebrates the Centenary by consecrating St Mary's—in Latin, of course.

These are comfortable, even triumphant, years for the Church. Vocations are strong. Six young Jesuits are ordained at St Mary's in this centennial year. The measures of Catholic faithfulness are clear. Sin-talk—venial and mortal—gives arithmetic to life. Every immoral act is a complete thing in itself: committed, examined, confessed, forgiven. Rules of fasting and abstinence, of Sunday Mass attendance, of sexual behaviour bring heaven and hell into the kitchen, the bedroom and everyone's body. The queues outside the confessionals are long on Saturday afternoons.

Devotions are prolific: First Fridays for the Sacred Heart, First Saturdays for Our Lady of Fatima. The Rosary with its 15 mysteries, the holidays of obligation bring the narrative of salvation and dogmatic declaration into everyday life. The Blessed Sacrament is a real presence that brings love and a little mysticism into the heart and soul. 40 Hours Devotions are intense; Corpus Christi processions, public acts of faith.

Public prayer tends to be mantra-like: the Latin Mass, the Rosary, Hail Mary, Our Father, the Creed. The mantra allows an inner freedom and privacy in devotion that is precious to the faithful. The transcendence of the divine is played out in the grandeur and solemnity of the liturgy. The catechism, known by rote, apologetics caught in the *Catholic Hour* on radio or in the Catholic Truth Society pamphlets stress the rationality of the faith. Magazines like *The Messenger* and the *Madonna* translate the rationality of the faith into human story. Fortress faith is reinforced by embargos on entry into Protestant and Anglican churches. Prayer with them is absolutely forbidden.

The hundredth year of the parish is something of a peak of the older church.

It is 2006. These 50 years have seen more change in the parish's living faith and worship than in any of its other 100. Vatican Council II asked the parish to see itself in a new light, as part of a Church that was on a pilgrimage through the mystery of God's love. Instead of holding on to a faith that was whole and frozen in time, the parish was asked to discover God's grace in every minute of its modern life. Instead of finding the real presence of Christ only in the tabernacle, the parish was asked to find Christ as well in those who stood beside them and, above all, in the poor and suffering. Faith is hard work. It doesn't come by decree or in the answers to questions in a catechism. It comes as a journeying through the histories made of God's love and Christ's saving action in scripture. Worship isn't passive spectatorship. It is active engagement of mind, body and soul in the theatre of salvation. Conscience isn't dumb obedience to rule. It is an exploration of a God-given freedom. The People of God aren't just the hierarchy, nor the parish just the parish priest. Governance is everybody's responsibility.

^ A new freedom and joy at communion
< And bread and wine.

The Church in Australia wasn't really ready for these changes, and many in the parish suffered in the years after Vatican II. These last 40 years have indeed been a pilgrimage. Experiments in parish governance haven't worked very well. But the discovery of a mode of worship with its appropriate language, the realisation that generational differences in believing require not just patience but love, the development of the theatre of the year's liturgy, and the enrichment of sacred spaces with colour and gesture and voice, the awareness that the parish is reflective as well as active, the demand that the Word that is preached must be intellectually satisfying as well as inspiring—all this has meant that the parish is a light on the hill that is seen for many kilometres around.

v Words, colour, images—living worship.
< Balloons rising into the sky—an Easter spectacular.

^ Tom Costelloe SJ at Mass.

^ Paul Coleman SJ and Friend.

^ Bob Walsh SJ baptising.

> Peter Quin SJ waiting.

< Paul Coleman SJ being ordained at St Mary's.

ᵛ The young being confirmed in their priestliness.

PRIESTLINESS

∧ Consecration at a concelebrated Mass.

∨ Henry Johnston SJ, parish priest, 1954–1956, and author of the centenary history *A Seed that Grew*.

There would have been few among the 133 priests who have served the parish through 150 years who did not believe that they were called by God to be a priest, and who would not have prayed long hours to discover whether 'they had a vocation', as the phrase went. Their first Masses with their first blessings would have been a joyful, holy experience for all. In their secret hearts they would have savoured the pleasure of dressing-up in vestments. The respect that their clerical collar gave them should have humbled them.

As all but two of these 133 were Jesuits, they would have been hard put to separate the priesthood from all that made up the Jesuit life. There used to be a saying that 'ordination was a reward for a life well spent' for a Jesuit. Nearly all would have spent 14 or 15 years in preparation for the priesthood, and another two to finish it off with final examinations that would determine if they could take high office in the Society, and a third year of novitiate in which they made the 30-day Spiritual Exercises of Ignatius Loyola again. Most of them would

have spent three or four years teaching as 'scholastics' in Jesuit schools. For the rest of their lives they would entertain one another with stories of the bizarre and human events of these 17 years. Jesuits have a love of theatre. There is much theatre in community life.

Their sense of theatre would become a pastoral tool for them to read, then make story, of the lives around them. Priests are close witnesses to death and disaster, injustice and cruelty. They bury the dead, baptise the newly born. They marry young lovers. They salve the wounds of divorce. They must translate what they see to give hope to others.

Jesuits take a vow of poverty, chastity and obedience. Their poverty won't be pressing, but it will always humble them to seek permission for this or that. Their chastity will require carefulness that any man would find hard. They have to discover how the absence of love in their life doesn't make them hard. They urge community on the parish, and sometimes find it difficult to make community among themselves. Obedience will cut deep when they have given all to one parish, only to be told to go to another.

They won't be able to preach the Word of God, unless they are prayerful and reflective men. It will always be difficult not to let their worship wrinkle into ritualism. They must nourish their spirits with constant reading.

More than half these Jesuits were born in Ireland, and until the 1930s all were trained in Ireland or Europe. The first Australian-born (Adelaide) parish priest was Richard O'Mara SJ 1929–1947. For 45 years he walked the North Shore. He was one of the great builders of the parish and paid for his building with housie, boxing matches and dance competitions. His successor, Arthur Stone SJ, 1947–1953, was the first really homegrown product of the parish.

^ Arthur Stone SJ, parish priest St Mary's, 1948–1953.

He was educated in the Marist Brother's school in the parish. Indeed he converted to Catholicism as a boy there. He was an engineer and a player of first-grade rugby league for North Sydney (surely a great pastoral advantage!) before joining the Jesuits. He was a man for all seasons — a fan of Johnny Ray against episcopal advice — and all faiths, being ecumenical long before it was fashionable.

An important period for the parish began in 1971, when James Dynon SJ was made parish priest (1971–1974). He was the first of what became a continual line to today of Jesuits trained in philosophy and theology at Loyola College, Watsonia, and at Canisius College, Pymble, to come to the parish. They belong to an exciting period of Jesuit history in Australia. They are educated to the Church that Vatican Council II would make, long before the Council. They put an Australian stamp on Jesuitry.

Very few of the 131 Jesuits in the parish were trained for parishes. Almost all are diverted from the educational apostolate of the Jesuits to the parishes. But in the 1970s the Spirit struck the Province hard in the person of the Jesuit General Pedro Arrupe SJ.

Hear what he says to them:

At the risk of startling you, let me tell you quite honestly: it is not this new world [of religious change] that I fear. After all God is there—however difficult it may be at times to discover Him. I am rather afraid that we Jesuits have little or nothing to offer this world, little or nothing to say or do that would justify our existence as Jesuits. I am afraid that we may repeat yesterday's answers to tomorrow's problems, talk in a way men no longer understand, speak a language that does not speak to the heart of living man. If we do this, we shall more and more be talking to ourselves; no one would listen, because no one will understand what we are trying to say!

That inspired the Australian Jesuits to create a Pastoral Ministry Gathering to formulate a mission statement for all the Australian Jesuit parishes. Paul Coleman SJ, George Belfrage SJ and Celso Romanin SJ of the North Shore parishes helped formulate policies that breathed life into the parish.

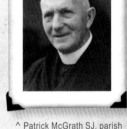

^ Patrick McGrath SJ, parish priest Lavender Bay, 1932–1943.

Of course, Vatican Council told us that priestliness belonged to all the People of God, not just to the priests. Those young people standing there with the stoles of their priestliness over their shoulders at their confirmation will take the parish on the next steps of the Pilgrim Church.

^ John O'Shaughnessy SJ, parish priest Lavender Bay, 1950–1953, with St Francis Xavier pupils.

< Sisters Eulalie Artup RSM and Aloysius Norris were familiar figures on North Sydney streets. Courtesy Mercy Archives.

> Mary MacKillop RSJ, c.1875, aged about 33 years. Courtesy Congregational Archives RSJ.

Perhaps no one has served the parish as well in its 150 years as those hundreds of young women and men who heard the Lord's message to the rich young man: 'If you wish to be perfect, go and sell what you own, and give the money to the poor, and you will have treasure in heaven; then come, follow me'. (Mt 19:21) 'Being perfect' would be a lifetime goal for them—in poverty, chastity and obedience.

Centuries of monasticism have given them firm guidelines for their lives. Whether in choir or in abbreviated form, they would pray the 'hours' of the day. They would wear a habit, every part of it being symbolic of something in their

^ Sisters Bertram, Columbkille, Carmel, Veronica and Dorotheus RSM, St Francis Xavier's School. Courtesy Stanton Library.
> The Reception Ceremony for novices in the Sisters of Mercy. Courtesy Mercy Archives.
>> First year of the Xavier Institute of Sister Formation 1967–1975, Lavender Bay. Courtesy Mercy Archives.

spiritual lives and apostolate. They would live in convents or 'houses', – whether cloistered or not, always a space of rules. Outside their convent they would always be accompanied. They would be closely regulated in their contact with family.

After a century in the parish, these sisters and brothers were icons of catholicity. The faithful, in a sense, owned them. They were the Church in their habits, in their lives of sacrifice. There would not have been a parishioner who did not incorporate into their life story some story of a sister's or a brother's eccentricities. There was probably not a boy or a girl who was not teased by the question, 'Do I have a vocation?'

When Vatican II called on the religious especially to be the 'light on the hill' in the Church's renewal, the sisters and brothers responded more positively and immediately than any part of the Church. They bore the brunt of the consternation of the faithful at all the changes. Their personal lives, not their habits, were now the sign of their commitment. Better educated than many of their priests, and more in tune theologically than the faithful, they took leadership in a changing Church. Free now, where they had been forbidden until 1967, to take postgraduate studies in all fields of theology, they (with many young laity following their example) became the chief force for reform in the Church. Many of them found it uncomfortable to be out in front, even of popes.

^ The first professed Sisters of St Joseph on the North Shore. Courtesy Congregational Archives RSJ.

^ Sister Ignatius Harding RSM, Mater Misericordiae Hospital. Courtesy Mercy Archives.

^ Novices, Sisters of St Joseph, Mount Street, pre-1900. Courtesy Congregational Archives RSJ.

^ Pope John Paul II leaves Blessed Mary MacKillop's Shrine with Sister Mary Cresp, Congregational Leader of the Sisters of St Joseph, 1986. Courtesy Congregational Archives RSJ.

^ The Grail, an international movement of women pursuing an apostolate of information and justice. The Grail has been part of parish life since 1936. Courtesy The Grail.

With great variety in their religious traditions, the sisters came to the parish. The Sisters of Mercy arrived first in 1875. Sr Ignatius McQuoin RSM had brought them to Sydney from Liverpool ten years before. They came to West Street seeking some respite from their gruelling work among the destitute. They stayed to educate the poor and well-off alike at Monte Sant' Angelo, St Francis Xavier's, St Mary's Primary School, to heal the sick at Mater Hospital, and to help all religious women in the archdiocese through the changes of Vatican II at the Xavier Institute, Lavender Bay. Mercy convents in these years before their federation were always independent of one another. The Goulburn Mercies brought their ministry of hospitality to 'Mercedes', the former home of the Cahill family on Walker Street, in 1943.

Blessed Mary MacKillop established a novitiate for her Sisters of St Joseph in 1884. Dean Kenny had given them his 'Alma Cottage'. Her sisters taught at Mount Street, St Francis Xavier's and St Mary's. Blessed Mary's extraordinary efforts to establish a religious congregation appropriate to Australian conditions is a story parishioners should know. Make a pilgrimage to her shrine on Mount Street, and search it out.

Inspired by the heroics of the Catholic Counter-Reformation, Mary Ward founded the Loreto Sisters (Institute of the Blessed Virgin Mary) to educate young women. The Loretos came to the North Shore at Normanhurst in 1897, then to Milson's Point and Kirribilli by slow expansion between 1901 and 1975; Mother Philomena Heaton IBVM gave a lifetime of service to the parish from 1901 to 1963.

The Missionary Sisters of the Society of Mary, with missions in the Pacific, Australia and Bangladesh, established themselves in Walker Street Lavender Bay (1977–99). There they made a place of retreat and prayer. The Benedictine Adorers of the Sacred Heart of Jesus, known as the Tyburn Nuns, set up a chapel of Perpetual Adoration on Berry Street (1958–62), but the construction of the Warringah Expressway forced them to Manly.

'The Marist Brothers of the Schools' have proudly preserved the traditions of their founder, Saint Marcellin Champagnat (1789–1840), to influence all facets of student's lives for 118 years in the parish. Michael Kelly SJ, the parish priest, had invited them into the parish in 1884. He provided a residence for them on the parish grounds and paid the fares for three brothers to come from Europe. The boys of the school have constantly enriched the spiritual life of the parish with their creative liturgies.

In 1936, 'The First Five' of the Grail came from Holland, where the Church had great vision of what religious experience would need to be for the rest of the millennium and on. The Grail was not a religious congregation in the traditional sense. It was an international movement of young, old, single and married women prepared to conduct a modern apostolate of information — for example, justice, ecology, indigenous peoples, liberation theology, Muslims and East Timor. By wandering pilgrimage, they ended up at 'Avila' on McHatten Street.

The sisters, depleted in numbers in the 1970s and '80s and seeking new apostolates in that time of change after Vatican II, seeded what was to bring the real aggiornamento in the parish: the Pastoral Ministry.

WOMEN

In 1962, John XXIII urged the Church to reflect on the 'signs of the times' to discover God's Providence in the world. All nature is graced, he implied. One of the 'signs of the times' John XXIII urged the Church to notice was the growing awareness of the inequality between women and men and the instruments of power, most notably language, used to sustain that inequality. For centuries the Church had been seen as the 'perfect society'. But it wasn't. God has no gender. There is 'neither male nor female in Christ'.

Listening ...

The first steps towards women's equality in the Church were small: on to the altar, into ministries, inclusive language. But it would be one step forward, two steps back. On to the altar, but not into the pulpit to preach, let alone to the priesthood; into the ministries, but not into orders; extravagant exclusive language adjusted, but no effort to change the patriarchal metaphors that suffuse Catholic religious experience. Women and men are complementary in nature, the Popes teach, but not equal. Ominously now there are attempts to silence reflective debate and retreat into a notion of a pure Church unpolluted by 'signs of the times'.

The parish resolved many of these issues by a 'just-do-it' approach that made the new freedoms of women in ritual, worship and decision-making seem natural. But more importantly, the parish discovered a way in which

Laughing ...

∨ Women's Spirituality Nights.
A thousand women ...

> On the altar, graced nature, sneakers and all.

equality was something more than a political struggle. If women were prevented from preaching from the pulpit, then women's lives could be made sacramental in the stories they tell of their spiritual journeying. If they were denied priesthood, they could act out their priestliness by letting others enter into their spirit by speaking to the whole body as well as the mind, by revealing what was actual in their religious experiences, not what 'should be', by being womanly in the presence of a thousand women. For ten years, Women's Spirituality Nights have given hope. In the words of the theologian Letty Russell, by 'making a memory of the future', they would 'subvert the Church into being a Church'.

^ Proclaiming the Gospel.

^ Michael Paxton, Pastoral Assistant, ministering.

^ Easter.

˅ Sister Janette Quade RSM of the 'Flying Squad', Lavender Bay.

^ Ministry of Youth with Caroline Jones.
> Rite of Christian Initiation for Adults.
>> Prayers of the Faithful.

Younger parishioners accustomed to the ordinariness today of the Eucharistic ministry, or of hearing a woman read the scriptures, or of seeing their liturgies crafted by young people in jeans, won't realise how extraordinary these scenes are for those who grew up in a Church of different times. Carlo Caretto once wrote: 'The Eucharist is the weakness of God, the silence of God.' It has been an awesome experience for those of earlier times and who are not priests to open the tabernacle, to take communion to those cruelly hit by stroke. To stand before a line of believers, each with different life experiences, each saying 'Amen' to that extravagant proposition 'The Body of Christ', is to experience something of the weakness of God, the silence of God, in oneself.

That the priestliness of Christ belonged to all who were baptised in Christ, that all like Christ were not to be ministered to, but were to minister, was one of the more revolutionary declarations of Vatican II. It was a call to revive the work of the Spirit in the early Church, where all were ministers to all.

So there is a richness in the parish that wasn't there 40 years ago—a Eucharistic ministry, a ministry of healing, a ministry of family worship, a ministry of prayer and meditation, a ministry of catechesis, a ministry of compassion, a ministry of music, a ministry of initiation in the faith—to name just a few.

Such multiplicity of ministries needs guidance through reflection, and organisation through administration. A major step in the evolution of the parish into a Pilgrim Church was the employment of professional Pastoral Assistants in the 1980s. Their prayerful Thursday meetings together with the priests give them the reflective strength that comes from many perspectives. They shape the coming weekend liturgies then and discover ways the Jesuit resources of scriptural and theological expertise and insights into the social issues of the day can be put to the use of the parish. The Pastoral Teams constantly survey the parish for its spiritual needs. Dialogue, Vatican II believed, was the best instrument of renewal. The Pastoral Teams are in constant dialogue among themselves and with the parish.

Archbishop Oscar Romero, the San Salvador martyr, wrote a reflection on ministries: 'We are prophets of a future not our own'.

Hope is the true grace of ministries never done.

COMPASSION

^ The Men of the Parish, St Francis Xavier's, c.1934. There were many stalwarts of compassion among them in these trying years of unemployment and depression. Frank Cox is there in the back row. He features in the parish's history as a man of wisdom and charity. He was educated here at St Francis Xavier's and at the Marist Brothers North Sydney. He tells in his oral history in the North Sydney Council archives how the building of, and then the employment in, Luna Park was the saving of many families. He was proud of his Papal Cross, but even prouder to be made an Acolyte at age 76. He was a constant Visitor of the Hospitals and Homes for the Aged. He joined the St Vincent de Paul Society when he saw its compassion at work in the depression and never left it. The parish owes him much.

Liturgy makes justice by inspiring us to compassion. Compassion is the giving of ourselves — the things we own, the talents we have and the time we have to use them — to those less fortunate than ourselves. Liturgy makes justice by making us holy, giving us courage to change the world in some way for the better.

Compassion helps us do the hard things we would not ordinarily do.

Like: joining the Vincent de Paul Society, founded by Blessed Frederick Ozanam in 1833, and working the streets of Surry Hills among the truly poor, and collecting monies from what you think to be the most generous parish in Australia.

Like: spending the Sunday nights for which the parish is responsible among the homeless at Theresa House in Redfern, and working as usual on Monday.

Like: being part of the Lavender Bay 'Flying Squad', comforting the aged and lonely, caring for the children of single parents, caring for refugees from Vietnam and the world-over.

Like: spending days, weeks, months, years working for the Australian Jesuit Mission.

Like: responding generously, in money terms, to the almost weekly appeals for help.

We have to be educated to compassion. Each week ministers create Prayers of the Faithful that remind us of

a need — reconciliation, refugees in detention centres, victims of tsunami, wise governance. The liturgy itself is a great educator — in its readings, in the theatre of Christ's sacrifice, in the seasons of the year, in the communion of saints whose heroics we celebrate, in the witness of the priests in their homilies.

At Lavender Bay there is a reminder of the sort of compassion social justice and charity require. It is the Leo XIII Building, formerly the parish school, then the Xavier Institute. Now it is the home of the Catholic Commission for Justice and Peace, and Caritas. Leo XIII's encyclical *Rerum Novarum* (1891) and Pius X's *Quadragesimo Anno* (1931) spoke to the Australian Catholic working class, if not in terms of the popes' conservatism, then on how the Australian workers' struggle for social justice might have a Catholic philosophical/theological foundation. The Australian bishops' annual Social Justice Statements have, since 1940, been the way in which compassion through social justice has had an Australian dimension. The parish has had, through one of its priests, Frank Brennan SJ, a way of educating itself on indigenous social issues, and through one of its parishioners, Dr Michael Costigan, executive secretary of the Bishops' Committee of Justice, Development, Ecology and Peace for 17 years, an expert commentator on Social Justice Statements.

Emmet Costello SJ would say, there's no compassion and no promotion of justice without love.

REMEMBERING VIRTUES OLD AND CELEBRATING VIRTUES NEW

The early morning weekday Mass, 6.00 am or 6.30 am with its daily communicants was, and is, a sign of the Spirit at work. The church is silent and still. One of the congregation quietly lights the candles, prepares the gifts. The Jesuit priest will have risen an hour or so before to complete his morning meditation or to begin the saying of his office. These days Father Tom O'Donovan SJ says the 6.30 am Mass. His pastorate is to the sick and aged. He says Mass and anoints the sick in the Sacrament of Healing every month in the Brothers' Residence. He is in much demand for funerals and is careful to find the right words for the occasion. He ministers to those more comfortable with older devotions. He has long had the custom of leaving a diary on a small offering table in the church. There, in the always-blue ink pen, the early Mass goers inscribe their intentions for the Mass. It is a daily ritual of much meaning. See how he divides the day's intentions into three: 'Sick, Suffering, Sorrowing', 'Need Our Prayers', 'Deceased'. You can see, also, how crowded and overwritten it becomes each day with names and thoughts. It is a little book deep with memories.

^ The loving acceptance of their children's calling to the Church was a gift in faith, hope and charity of many parents. Alice Mungoven beside Sister M. Dorotheus RSM and two of the first vocations from St Francis Xavier's School, Sister M. Colette RSM and Sister Kathleen Robertson RSM.

v The Blue Book for the 6.30am Mass.

A parish needs to have memories and places to record them:

Of families born, married, buried in the parish, with children they gave to the church. Some of them: William and Bridget Cahill, Joseph and Mildred Trubidy, four generations of the Bellews, Reg and Gwen Mitchell, Pat and Olive McRobie.

Of tireless workers and leaders. Some of them: Frank Cox, Thomas and Alice Mungoven, Eileen Madden, Tess Fitzgerald, Pat Jenkins, Clarrie Smith, Frank Day, Fred and Ethel Scorer.

A parish needs to celebrate those who share their wisdom and give their energy to many projects:

Some of them: Paul and Rosemary Flannery, Caroline Jones, John and Margaret Slattery, Joan Ward, Margaret and Peter Rush, Ida Cameron, Michael O'Dea, Norma Boyle, Bill Nichols, Dennis Goggin, Jim Egan, Therese Delanty, Yvonne Quarrell, Bill and Josephine Gibbons, Biddy Kennedy (and her late husband Noel), Philippa Green, Des and Joan Giffney, Jim (R.I.P.) and Iris L'Estrange, Kerry Bristow, the Collins Family, Jim Cahill, Mark Quarrell, Peter Taniane, Bob Hanley.

^ Joy, chaos and innocence on the altar.
Photo Robyn Treseder.

^ Choir 1913.

^ Choir 2005.

It is the 9.00 am Family Mass at St Mary's. The children who will dramatise the scripture readings are rehearsing. The choir is practising. There is a joyful sort of chaos, the aisles already beginning to have small bodies crawling this way and that, parents separating the young from the older children. Classes 2 and 4 of St Mary's Primary School are performing today's liturgy, and the Bristow family is welcoming us. 'Gather us in, the lost and forsaken. Gather us in, the lame and the blind', the choir leads us joyfully and hopefully. A 6- or 7-year-old school-age soloist sings 'Lord have mercy!' We clap the Alleluia. A young girl triumphantly processes the Book of the Gospels. 1 Samuel 26: 2–23: David's theft of Saul's spear, yet refusal to take advantage of his helplessness, provides plenty of drama for the young readers. Dozens bring up the gifts. For the canon (do we use that word these days?) of the Mass, children of all sizes crowd around the altar. It is a brilliant scene, with Tony Smith SJ, the new parish priest, in his green vestments in the middle.

He is easy with the children, even if he is shyly awkward with the gestures that accompany the songs. There is a little scurry as a small girl knocks down a candle. But there are plenty of doctors in this congregation, and all is well. Communion is crowded and natural. The very young are blessed with the host.

The ritual of this Mass is crowded, as every ritual is, with piecemeal experiences: of noise and song, of distractions and seconds of prayerfulness, of microphones that don't work, of children getting out of hand, of movement and moments of stillness. But we humans are adept at reducing the complexities of our ritual to simple meanings. As we sing our recessional, we feel at peace with ourselves and sense the real presence of Christ in his Spirit among us in a real world.

The parish has the right in its sesquicentenary year to celebrate the Gifts of the Spirit that have come to it through its Pastoral Assistants. May the grace of the Lord go with them: John Raper and Carmen Murphy (Rest in Peace), Michael Paxton, Genine D'Arcy, Michael Murphy, Jennifer Kos and those who preceded them: Sisters Clare Koch RSJ, Marlene Hixon FMM, Margaret Culhane RSJ, Kathleen Robertson RSM, Loretta Rossen OSU, Sheila MacNamara PBVM, Jenny Gilligan FMM, Elen Cahill RSM.

^ Danielle Joosse and her Ministry of Music.

^ 'May Yahweh Bless you and keep you', they sing. Indeed.

The 'Irish Bishops' in Australia in the 1880s were anxious that the Church was becoming too 'methodistic' with too much hymn singing and too much English in its worship. But the parishioners of St Mary's and Star of the Sea, Milson's Point, were always proud of their choirs and maestros. The singing of the choirs tended to be a performative art both socially and liturgically, except, perhaps, when the faithful could let themselves loose on 'Faith of Our Fathers' or 'Tantum Ergo' at Benediction.

In 1903, Pius X determined that Gregorian and polyphony, such as Palaestrina, were the appropriate music for Catholic worship. Instruments other than the organ were frowned on. Catholic awkwardness in singing became proverbial. Henry Johnston SJ, parish priest 1954–1956 and a Gregorian enthusiast, was known to prowl the aisles pushing hymnbooks under the noses of the more reluctant singers. The liturgical reforms of the 1950s (dialogue Masses, returning the Easter Saturday ceremonies to their appropriate time) brought with them a renewed excitement to produce quality music for the liturgy. Young Jesuit theologians from Canisius College inspired by the world figure in liturgical music, Joseph Gelineau SJ, would perform the Easter ceremonies and create paraliturgies for the young at St Francis Xavier's. Instruments such as tympanies and trumpets made a first and bold appearance at these paraliturgies.

Vatican Council II called for full, conscious and active participation of the People of God in their worship. At St Francis Xavier's, under the leadership of Josephine Gibbons, the response came in the form of a Folk Mass. The evolution of the 6.00 pm Sunday Mass at Lavender Bay and the development of some five or six musical styles in the different churches at different Masses has been one of the great musical triumphs in the parish.

In the 1960s, the guitar was king. Singing nuns and friars were an Australian and global phenomenon. Protest singing in peace demonstrations showed how body and soul could be engaged in communal action. But 'Blowin' in the wind', 'He's got the whole world in his hand', 'Kumbaya' were just an entry point into a new musical experience for the Church. Many would have agreed with the young Dr Joseph Ratzinger, now Pope Benedict XVI, that they craved a more transcendental experience in the art and beauty of their music than mere 'utility'.

But the community—loyal and many—learned, by just doing it, to sing their liturgy, and to discover thereby their own deep memories beyond words and musical scores. Authentic worship touches on the mysteries of death, of life, of forgetting, of loving, of losing and gaining again.

The ministry of music is a prophetic ministry, dreaming to shape the future with insight and wisdom. In the words of William Bauman, 'It uncritically respects the individual taste, and life choices of the persons served, freeing them to create themselves anew. It urges, inspires, shows support; it never forces.'